Fligh

Contents

 # Features

WORD BUILDER

Would you like to travel somewhere nice and warm when the weather turns cold? Learn what the word *migrate* means on page 5.

Instead of a scarecrow, some people now use a machine called a bird scarer to keep birds out of their crops. Turn to page 9 for more.

WHAT'S YOUR OPINION?

FACT FINDER

Discover how many birds and other animals you know in a wildlife refuge. Be a **Nature Detective** on page 14.

Some people say that snow geese bring the summer sun to the icy Arctic. Find out more about the life cycle of these birds on page 20.

IN FOCUS

SITESEEING · PLANTS & ANIMALS ·

Why do some birds become extinct?

Visit www.rigbyinfoquest.com
for more about **BIRDS IN DANGER.**

Signs of the Seasons

Many birds are expert travelers. They often have two homes—a summer home and a winter home. Flying long distances, the birds travel, or migrate, from one home to another.

In autumn, when the days grow cooler and food begins to run out, the birds leave their summer home. They migrate to another part of the world where the days are warmer and there is plenty of food. When the weather changes there, the birds migrate back again. The coming and going of the birds signals the changing seasons.

The word *migrate* comes from the Latin word *migrare*, meaning "to move from one place to another—to change."

Many animals migrate. Some, such as birds and whales, travel from one end of Earth to the other and back again each year.

Most migrating birds use a few main **flyways.** Scientists believe that birds use landmarks, such as mountains and coastlines, or the positions of the sun, moon, and stars to find their way.

5

Feather Power

Different kinds of birds migrate in different ways. Some fly alone. Some fly in large flocks. Small birds often fly during the cool of the night. Other birds fly only during the day. Some birds land now and then to rest, while others complete their long journey without stopping.

No matter how migrating birds travel, these feathered creatures have got what it takes to complete some of the world's most surprising journeys.

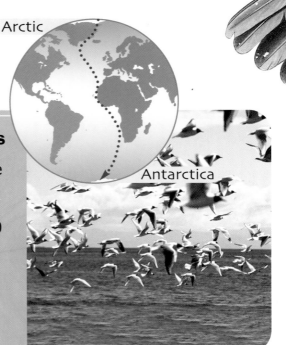

Arctic

Antarctica

Record Breakers

Arctic terns migrate farther than any other bird. They travel about 11,000 miles from their nests in the Arctic to their winter getaway in Antarctica.

The Inside Story

Bones

Flight feathers

Heart

Lungs

1. Bones: hollow, light, strong
2. Flight feathers: light, smooth, strong
3. Heart: two pumps to move blood
4. Lungs: small, with deep air sacs

A Bird's-Eye View

Not so long ago, migrating birds flew over a vast land of rivers, forests, marshes, and rich feeding grounds. The view birds have today is a very different one. In many places, people have dammed rivers, drained wetlands, built cities, and turned forests into farmland.

Sometimes, however, birds can eat the leftovers of a crop harvest. Some farmers allow flocks of migrating birds to eat dropped grain after crops are harvested.

Bird Scarers—Good or Bad?

I think bird scarers are bad. They are noisy machines that give birds no peace at all. Migrating birds need to eat and rest. Surely people can spare some food.

I think bird scarers are good. They keep birds away from crops the farmer hasn't harvested. The birds still get to eat leftovers, but the farmer can make a living and provide food for people.

Resting and Refueling

There are safe places in which migrating birds and other animals can eat and rest. Many countries around the world have set aside huge areas of land as wildlife **refuges.** These cover millions of miles, from Arctic tundra to deserts, wetlands, and tropical forests. They help provide food, water, shelter, and space for many **endangered** animals.

Secretary bird

Canada geese

Scientists use radar and satellite tracking systems, along with bird banding, to better understand and take care of endangered or **threatened** birds.

Heron

Whooping cranes

A Wildlife Refuge

Bosque del Apache is one of the most amazing wildlife refuges in North America. On the edge of desert lands and bordering the great Rio Grande, this vast refuge is home to thousands of birds. These include Arctic geese, ducks, wading birds, and sandhill cranes.

During autumn, the air is filled with the honking of wild geese and the cries of cranes as flock after flock circles and lands. These birds fly into the refuge's wooded wetlands each winter. They share the habitat with many other birds, mammals, reptiles, and amphibians.

Porcupine
Sandhill crane
Deer
Bullfrog
Coyote
Goose
Rattlesnake
Stilt

Bosque del Apache

Key

🏠	Visitors' center
📶	Viewing platform
🚶	Nature trail
🚲	Bikes allowed
〰️	Marsh area
🚜	Crops
〜	Waterway

Nature Detective

FACT FINDER

Here are some animals you might see in the Bosque del Apache wildlife refuge. How many can you find and name?

Check your detective skills here!

1. Mule deer
2. Bald eagle
3. Bats
4. Porcupine
5. Sandhill cranes
6. Coyote
7. Pheasant
8. Whooping cranes
9. Turkey
10. Squirrel
11. Blue heron
12. Snow geese
13. Crane chicks
14. Rabbit
15. Quail
16. Rattlesnake
17. Snowy egret
18. Mallard ducks
19. Bullfrog
20. Mouse

15

Bird-Watchers

People from near and far visit refuges to observe birds. Bird-watchers identify and **classify** different kinds of birds. They record bird sounds and study bird behavior. Their findings often help the people who work to protect birds and their habitats.

Dawn is one of the best times to watch birds. Flocks often rest still and quiet on or near water in the dark of night. As the sun begins to rise, hundreds of birds suddenly take to the air. The sky can be filled with the sound of beating wings and the cries of wild birds on the move.

Bird-Watching Tips

• Keep your distance from wildlife. Watch from a **blind.**

• Arrive in the early morning or the late afternoon when wildlife is most active.

• Leave only footprints and take only memories and pictures.

The Snow Geese

The honking of thousands of wild geese is a sound not many people forget. About 23,000 snow geese migrate south from the icy Arctic to spend each winter in the warmth of New Mexico. In spring, they journey once more to the Arctic land where they were born. The Inuit people there say that the birds bring the summer sun with them. To many native people across North America, these white birds of winter are a symbol of the seasons and the cycles of nature.

The journey of the snow geese begins in the wild environment of the Arctic. Here, during the brief far-northern summer, the geese make their nests and raise their chicks.

A goose and a gander stay together for life. Each goose in the flock lays a **clutch** of eggs. She warms, or **incubates**, the eggs for three weeks.

All the chicks in the colony hatch at the same time. They must leave their nests only six hours after hatching and follow their parents to the feeding grounds. Here, both adults and chicks eat and fatten to be ready for their 3,000-mile-long journey south. They have only six weeks in which to leave before the icy Arctic winter settles in.

These young, first-time fliers learn the flight paths from their parents as they migrate across the great forests of Canada toward New Mexico.

21

Operation Migration

When it comes to the migration of geese, Canadian inventor and bird lover Bill Lishman is an expert. Bill dreamed of flying with a flock of wild Canada geese, and he was a person who was determined to make his dream come true.

As a young man, Bill liked to build things. He also liked to hang glide. When a family of young geese lost their way and turned up on his farm, Bill decided to teach the birds to fly along beside him. His work with the geese is honored in the movie *Fly Away Home*.

Bill Lishman later began a wildlife organization called Operation Migration.

Operation Migration's current work is flying ultralights with a flock of cranes as they migrate south. A team of biologists, pilots, and veterinarians will help keep the cranes safe during their long journey.

Crane Care

The Operation Migration teams aren't the only ones who are helping birds. When scientist George Archibald learned that there were only 21 whooping cranes left in the world, he decided to try to save cranes from becoming **extinct**.

Young whooping cranes

With another scientist, George turned a farm into a crane conservation center and named it the International Crane Foundation. He got permission to raise cranes and then borrowed adult cranes from zoos around the world. Soon there were many chicks hatching!

ICF workers discovered that cranes learn by **imprinting.** If a human is the first thing a baby crane sees, it will think the human is its mother. It won't learn to act like a crane because it will try to act like the human. ICF workers now know to use crane puppets when caring for young birds.

Cranes hold a special place in the cultures of people around the world. Unlike most birds, cranes live for as long as twenty years in the wild. To some people, cranes are a symbol of long life.

There are many myths about cranes. Some say that the Greek alphabet was invented by watching the flight of cranes. Others believe that small birds migrated on the backs of cranes, and that the constant chattering of these little passengers kept the great birds entertained on their long journeys.

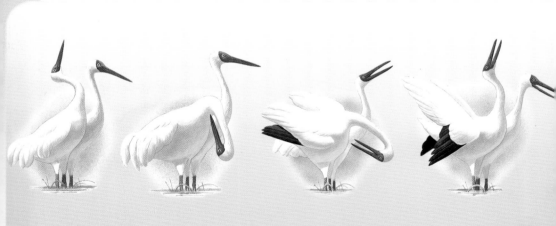

Cranes dance to attract a mate, and the pair stay together for life. The dancing of cranes has inspired human dances in many parts of the world.

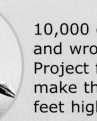

10,000 children from around the world drew pictures and wrote peace poems during the World Peace Project for Children in 1999. Their work was used to make the World's Largest Paper Crane. It was 120 feet high and over 215 feet from wing tip to wing tip!

Black-crowned crane

Sandhill crane

Blue crane

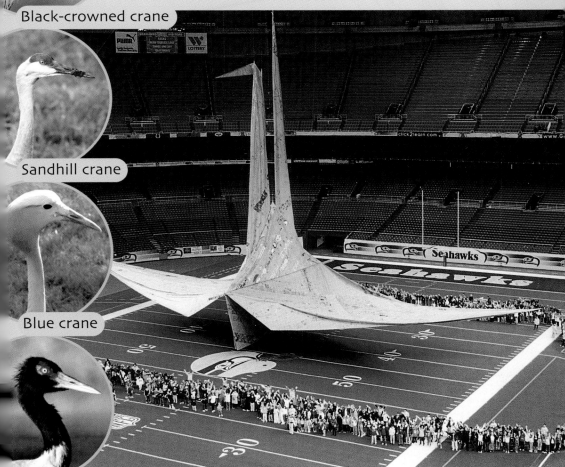

Black-necked crane

Why do some birds become extinct?

Visit www.rigbyinfoquest.com
for more about **BIRDS IN DANGER.**

Backyard Boosters

Anyone can help birds. Even if you live in the city, you can make your backyard or balcony a bird-friendly place by putting up a bird feeder, a birdbath, or a simple nesting box.

Many kinds of birds make their homes in the city, but cities also attract many migrating birds. These visitors can face dangers in a city, such as crashes with cars and power lines or attacks from cats.

It is always good to know where the closest bird-rescue center is in case you come to the rescue of an injured bird.

Peregrine falcons migrate from the Arctic to southern Europe, North America, and Asia. These great wanderers often nest on the ledges of city skyscrapers.

Glossary

blind – a hiding place. A blind blends into the background so that it is difficult to see.

classify – to sort or identify something and place it in a group or set

clutch – a group of eggs

endangered – very, very close to being the last one of a kind on Earth. Endangered plants and animals need human help to stay alive.

extinct – no longer living. If an animal is extinct, there are no more of that kind of animal alive.

flyways – the flight paths that many birds follow when they migrate from one place to another

imprinting – an almost instant way of learning that happens with some kinds of birds. Chicks learn how to behave by imprinting.

incubate – to keep eggs warm so they can hatch

refuges – special places that are set aside to provide food, shelter, and safety

threatened – close to being one of only a few left in the world

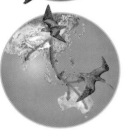

Index

Discussion Starters

1 Imagine you had to make a very long journey without stopping for food or shelter along the way. How would you prepare?

2 Birds are not the only animals that are losing their homes and feeding grounds to humans. What other animals with this problem can you think of? How could you find out more about the world's many threatened and endangered animals?

3 If you found an injured bird, what is the first thing you would do? How could you learn more about helping birds?